AF480939

Written & illustrated by Christiann MacAuley
stickycomics.com

ISBN 979-8-218-49230-4
First printing, September 2024

Published by Sticky Comics
Arlington, Virginia, United States

TABLE OF CONTENTS

0 Welcome
1 Career advice
2 Caffeine intake
3 Drinking + consequences
4 Almost a grownup
5 Food is friends you eat
6 Health & wellness is gonna kill me
7 Livin' that creative life
8 Tech obsession
9 Whatever

SO YOU'RE READING THIS BOOK

OMG. Thanks for picking up my first printed collection of comics. i'm super flattered you're here. Let me explain.

i started making what became "Sticky Comics" circa 2006 on sticky notes while i was trapped in my apartment working as a freelance designer. i had them all over my desk. As a person who compulsively starts new projects with zero plans, i started posting them on the internet, just because i could.

At first the sticky comics were a secret. Only my significant other, Jim, saw them, and he thought they were funny. Validation from loved ones was cool, but when strangers in other countries started following my work, i felt like i was onto something. i will always remember my first serious internet fan, Miguel in the U.K. Thanks, friend.

Over the years, my comics became popular enough to get attention around the internet. i got my first big Twitter celeb share (shout out to Ashton Kutcher) and eventually my work was licensed by some well-known brands (thanks, Tampax) and commissioned by publications like Cosmopolitan and BuzzFeed.

Sticky Comics has always been more of a collection of stuff than a series, and so this isn't a start-to-finish or even loosely chronological collection. instead, i picked common themes and grouped some of my work into them. Read it in any order. You'll see stylistic + coloring changes from comic to comic because i changed it up over time and tried new things. And it leaves out a lot of comics + topics that may appear in a future book.

Until now i've made hundreds of these comics, exhibited at comic cons + art shows, and continued my work in tech + design without ever publishing a book of this work. i have no good excuse for waiting so long. But i have to thank Jim, for being there to laugh with me the whole time, Sheridan, for all the encouragement and editing, and Ursa, for expecting me to get it done.

with love + bagels,
Christiann MacAuley
AKA sticky comics

PART 1
CAREER ADVICE

LET'S GET DRESSED FOR WORK

That moment when you forget to lie at the interview

it says here on page 17 of your resume that your "greatest strength is editing"
dude your doing so good
nod nod
Stickycomics.com

Right, i understand the work we delivered was half-assed. But you'll find in our agreement that we bill in quarter-ass increments.
stickycomics.com

"Personal Branding"? Does it hurt?
stickycomics.com

YOUR PROFITS AREN'T ETHICAL

MY ETHICS AREN'T PROFITABLE
Stickycomics.com

i USED TO GET R & R...

NOW i ONLY GET BRB

WE'RE HiRiNG RiSK-TAKERS!

WE HAD TO LET GO OF ALL THE ONES WE HAD
Christiann MacAuley • stickycomics.com

MEET HANDSY THE AI HAND, YOUR NEW AI ASSISTANT

i quit my job to start a career advice blog...
stickycomics.com

AND SO SHOULD YOU!

Christiann MacAuley
Stickycomics.com

"STOP SNORING, NICOLE — YOU'RE STILL ON THAT CONFERENCE CALL."

8 TYPES of KITCHEN SHARERS

sfickycomics.com

IT WAS THE WRONG THING
TO SAY TO THE GARDENER

WHY BE UNEMPLOYED?
WHEN YOU CAN BE A SELF-UNEMPLOYED...

STAY AT HOME CAT MOM

STREAMING MEDIA CRITIC

FANTASY REAL ESTATE INVESTOR

INDOOR PLANT SUPERVISOR

i WANT TO GET PAID TO DO SOMETHING i LOVE
i WANT TO GET PAID TO DO SOMETHING i LIKE
i WANT TO GET PAID TO DO SOMETHING i DON'T HATE
i WANT TO GET PAID TO DO SOMETHING
i WANT TO GET PAID TO DO NOTHING
stickycomics.com

Guru, i've grown rich and successful. i have all i ever wanted, but i feel unfulfilled.

Why do you seek MY advice?

You are a wise man with a long white beard, all alone on a mountaintop.

Then cast off your possessions, sit alone atop this mountain, watch your beard grow long & white, and you will know what i know.

sucker.
stickycomics.com

SO ROBOTS STOLE YOUR JOB. WHAT'S NEXT?

stickycomics.com

WHOA, LET'S NOT OVERTHINK THIS

LATER
UH, ARE YOU SURE YOU LOOKED AT THIS FROM EVERY ANGLE?
No.
Stickycomics.com

NETWORKING
IS THE WORST
sniff
sniff
stickycomics.com

PART 2
CAFFEINE INTAKE

iCED COFFEE

We're sweating together!

Christiann MacAuley • stickycomics.com

I DON'T LET MY FEELINGS CONTROL ME.
I ALREADY HAVE COFFEE FOR THAT.
stickycomics.com

COFFEE
is my naptime
stickycomics.com

MASLOW'S HIERARCHY OF NEEDS COFFEE
espresso
good coffee
coffee
caffeine
stickycomics.com

300
250
200
150
100
50
0
mg
COFFEE
TEA
RED BULL
COKE
MY BLOOD STREAM
AVERAGE CAFFEINE CONTENTS
stickycomics.com

"SLEEP"?

THAT'S LIKE COFFEE FOR PEOPLE WITH TOO MUCH FREE TIME
stickycomics.com

tea TOTALLY
stickycomics.com

i can't believe you're taking a picture of your latte.
Christiann MacAuley
Stickycomics.com

I AM BREWED IN EXTREME PRESSURE AS BOILING WATER IS FORCED THROUGH PRECISION-GROUND COFFEE BEANS IN A MATTER OF SECONDS!!
THAT'S COOL. I JUST, LIKE, SIT FOR A WHILE
stickycomics.com

i GOT UP PRETTY EARLY TODAY
DID YOU GET THE BEST WORM?

NO, THAT EARLY BIRD GOT IT

i NEVER SLEEP
stickycomics.com

stickycomics.com

PART 3
DRiNKiNG
(AND CONSEQUENCES)

the PB diet
PBJ
Pabst Blue Ribbon
the original hipster classic
PBR
CONSUME 4 to 6 UNITS OF EACH PB GROUP DAILY
stickycomics.com

GOOD KARMA DRINKING TIP

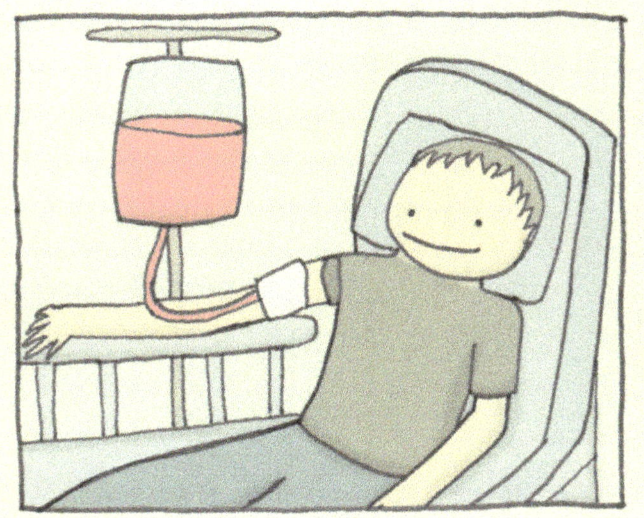 

GIVE BLOOD | CHUG A BEER

WHAT'S IN THE RED CUPS?

Stickycomics.com

"Say, Frank, why do we all wear suspenders? Did the 18th Amendment ban belts, too?"

I'LL HAVE A MIMOSA AND THE FRUIT & YOGURT PLATE
BRUNCH

ACTUALLY — MAKE THAT A BREAKFAST BURRITO

YEAH SURE I'LL TRY THE BLOODY MARY BAR

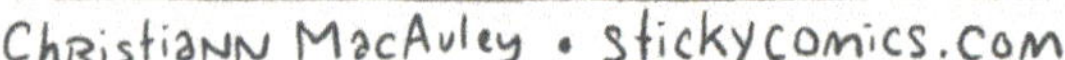

Christiann MacAuley • stickycomics.com

WHAT A BEAUTIFUL SUNSET!

BIG BUCK HUNTER
STEALS YOUR CHANGE

ACTUAL BUCK HUNTERS
STEAL YOUR SEATS

PLASTIC JUG VODKA

BARTENDER'S MOONSHINE

BATHROOM DOOR WON'T LOCK

...WHAT BATHROOM DOOR?

Christiann MacAuley • stickycomics.com

drink the best!

chug the rest.
el BARATO
stickycomics.com

"FIRST YOU TAKE
A DRINK,

THEN THE DRINK
TAKES A DRINK,

THEN THE DRINK
TAKES YOU."
stickycomics.com

stickycomics.com

stickycomics.com
EAT, DRINK AND BE MERRY...
FOR TOMORROW WE'LL HAVE A RAGING HANGOVER AND PRETEND IT'S FOOD POISONING

GODDAMMIT,
HARRY! YOU
SAID YOU'D
QUIT!

HUNGOVER AT 22
i want a breakfast burrito but i'd have to put on pants...

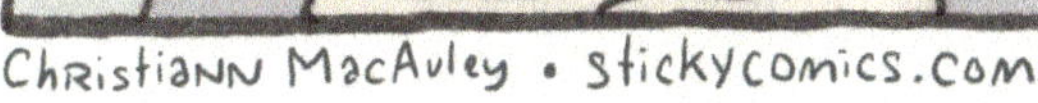

Christiann MacAuley • stickycomics.com

HUNGOVER AT 32
BRUNCH?! i'm still trying to hold down this coconut water
COCO

OH GOD, HUNGOVER ON EASTER...

THIS MUST BE HOW JESUS FELT.
stickycomics.com

Good Morning!
oh shit.
TEQUILA
stickycomics.com

PART 4
ALMOST A
GROWNUP

i AM A TERRIBLE ADULT.

i LOVE MOVING!
ROMPERS + HORSEY SHIRTS
BIKINI BOTTOMS
UNMATCHED SOCKS
TEA
DVDS

IT'S THE ONLY WAY i CAN KEEP MY HOUSE CLEAN.
OMPERS + ORSEY SHIRTS
BIKINI BOTTOMS
UNMATCHED SOCKS
stickycomics.com

i ALWAYS CHASE MY DREAMS!

BUT THEN i WAKE UP ANYWAY
stickycomics.com

CHINESE DELIVERY because the only soup delivery is wanton soup
INSULTINGLY BEAUTIFUL DAY
ALARMINGLY DEPLETED GATORADE STASH
TOILET PAPER because you don't own a box of Kleenex
GRATUITOUS NETFLIX BINGE
WebMD
iLL-ADVISED WebMD SEARCH
SO. MUCH. TEA.
FISHING FOR SYMPATHY ON SOCIAL MEDIA
stickycomics.com
LIVING ALONE IS AWESOME
until you get sick and wish you still lived with your mom ♥

stickycomics.com
DO the DISHES
1 OFTEN ENOUGH THAT NO ONE SAYS YOU NEVER DO THEM
2 INFREQUENTLY ENOUGH THAT NO ONE EXPECTS YOU TO DO THEM ALL THE TIME
3 POORLY ENOUGH THAT NO ONE WANTS YOU TO DO IT EVERY TIME

i LITERALLY OWN 17 HOODIES

BUT i CAN'T GO ANYWHERE UNTIL THIS ONE'S CLEAN
stickycomics.com

ONE DAY, ALL THIS WILL BE YOURS.
stickycomics.com

van life in the 90s
I LIVE IN A VAN DOWN BY THE RIVER!
#vanlife now
So you have a VAN?!
by the RIVER?!
stickycomics.com

IT STINKS IN HERE...
stickycomics.com

IT STINKS LIKE HOME!

COOKIES FOR BREAKFAST!
childhood

SNACKS
COOKIES FOR BREAKFAST
PUSH
adulthood
stickycomics.com

MOMENTS IN BECOMING A GROWNUP

PART 5
FOOD iS JUST FRIENDS YOU EAT

i AM A TENDER AND ADORABLE CUPCAKE

MOVE OVER, BITCH

i'M A BAGEL, MOTHERFUCKERS.
stickycomics.com

GROCERIES
Nah

BROCERIES
Brah!
Stickycomics.com

BURRITO
KITCHEN
mmm, i love this place
it's just like eating over the sink at home
stickycomics.com

it's not pronounced
PHO as in BRO.
it's PHUH as in BRUH
Phở
stickycomics.com

facebook reactions
(to a burrito)

burritos are
awesome

no seriously i
would fucking
love a burrito

of course
i want guac

i ate the
whole thing

i can't possibly
eat a second
burrito

now i have to
go to the
fucking gym

BAD WINE PAIRING

stickycomics.com

ORANGE YOU GLAD
i DIDN'T SAY BANANA?
stickycomics.com
HA HA
HAHA HA!

stickycomics.com

FAKE-OUT YOGURT FLAVORS

why do i keep buying these by mistake?

banilla

strawbacon

plain-tain

beach

pea lime pie

CHEERIO!
CHEX YOU LATER!
stickycomics.com

PART 6
HEALTH & WELLNESS IS GONNA KILL ME

OMG i ATE
THE WHOLE THING
ME EATING A BURRITO

i think i can
i think i can
stickycomics.com
ME EATING A SALAD

WHAT'S IN THE GREEN JUICE?
organic apples
free-range kale
cage-free sea kelp
artisanal himalayan tree moss
reclaimed plutonium
Shrek
stickycomics.com

DAY ONE
i'm starting a week-long juice cleanse
DAY TWO
it's going AWESOME!
DAY THREE
wine is juice, right?
Stickycomics.com

stickycomics.com

i'M SORRY, FRANK...
iT'S DEFINITELY A TUMOR
stickycomics.com

WHERE BOOBS GO AFTER SURGERY

YOUR SINUSES
ARE MINE,
HUMAN
stickycomics.com

i WORK REALLY HARD TO STAY ON MY DiET

Certificate of Achievement
this is to certify that you
GREAT JOB!
WENT to the GYM THAT ONE TIME
stickycomics.com

PROBIOTICS
OK, WHO WANTS TO COLONIZE MY INTESTINES?!
ME!
ME!
ME!
ME!
ME!
ME!
ME!
ME!
ME!
ME!
ME!
ME!
ME!
ME!
ME!
ME!
stickycomics.com

i WAS SiCK ALL WEEKEND. COULDN'T EAT FOR DAYS.
THAT'S AWFUL!

... BUT i LOST FIVE POUNDS!
YOU LOOK AMAZING!
stickycomics.com

PART 7
LIVIN' THAT CREATIVE LIFE

ME SUFFERING FOR MY ART

↳ MY ART

MY POST GOT 4 MILLION LIKES!

WOW! ARE YOU GONNA QUIT YOUR JOB?

YEAH I'M GONNA RETIRE WITH MY 4 MILLION $0 BILLS
stickycomics.com

This art is great! You should get paid for it

LATER
You get paid for this? Well, it isn't ART
stickycomics.com

LET'S GET DRUNK AND WATCH NETFLIX
LET'S GET DRUNK AND MAKE COMICS
stickycomics.com
SO, WHERE DO YOU GET YOUR IDEAS?

i JUST MAKE THEM UP i GUESS
stickycomics.com

THEN
NEVER SELL OUT, MAN

LATER
WHO THE HELL ARE YOU?
MY INDIE SHOW
MY INDIE
Stickycomics.com

BEING CREATIVE

STUFF WRITERS DO

stickycomics.com

WRITEMARES

stickycomics.com

THE BLANK PAGE

and then
DANGLING PLOTLINES

RIP
Chapter
6
KILLING YOUR
DARLINGS

No.
REJECTION

"Someday, when i'm a famous author,
i'll hire someone to finish this terrible novel."

TAP
TAP
TAP

it's done.
my masterpiece.

...

i hate it
Stickycomics.com

HOW TO STOP DOING EVERYTHING LAST MINUTE

I FEEL GREAT!
EVERY DAY I'M TAKING A WALK
WRITING IN MY JOURNAL
READING A BOOK
COOKING MY OWN HEALTHY FOOD
SPENDING TIME WITH LOVED ONES
WORKING OUT
MEDITATING
AND STAYING HYDRATED!
WOW! HOW'S YOUR JOB GOING?
THEY FIRED ME.
I WASN'T GETTING ANYTHING DONE
Stickycomics.com

WE
BUY
GOLD

NEED CASH?
WE BUY HOUSES
1 · 800 · SELL · LOW

SELL US YOUR USED CAR

WE BUY
INDIE CRED

WE BUY
INDIE CRED
"fuckin' finally."

PART 8
TECH OBSESSION

An Update is Available For Your Computer

stickycomics.com

GADGET PARTY #1 * BY CHRISTIANN MACAULEY FOR BITE TV * WWW.BITE.CA

GADGET PARTY #2 * BY CHRISTIANN MACAULEY FOR BITE TV * WWW.BITE.CA

GADGET PARTY #3 * BY CHRISTIANN MACAULEY FOR BITE TV * WWW.BITE.CA

SIR, I'M AFRAID YOUR BATTERY TYPE IS VERY RARE. IF WE CAN'T FIND A COMPATIBLE DONOR IN TIME... WELL, YOU MAY NEED TO PREPARE FOR THE WORST.
stickycomics.com

HOW TO MAKE A PHONE HAND

i'll have my autocorrect
text your autocorrect
stickycomics.com

RELATIVE IMPORTANCE OF MOBILE PHONE WEIGHT

RELATIVE IMPORTANCE OF MOBILE PHONE WEIGHT WHEN I DROP IT ON MY FACE
stickycomics.com

WINDOWS USERS

MAC USERS

LINUX USERS

stickycomics.com

read the paper

stare at your phone

make smalltalk

stare at your phone

take a nap

stare at your phone

GOTTA GO GOTTA GO
BUT...
WHERE'S MY PHONE?
1 MINUTE LATER
FINALLY
BUT...
it's dead.
stickycomics.com

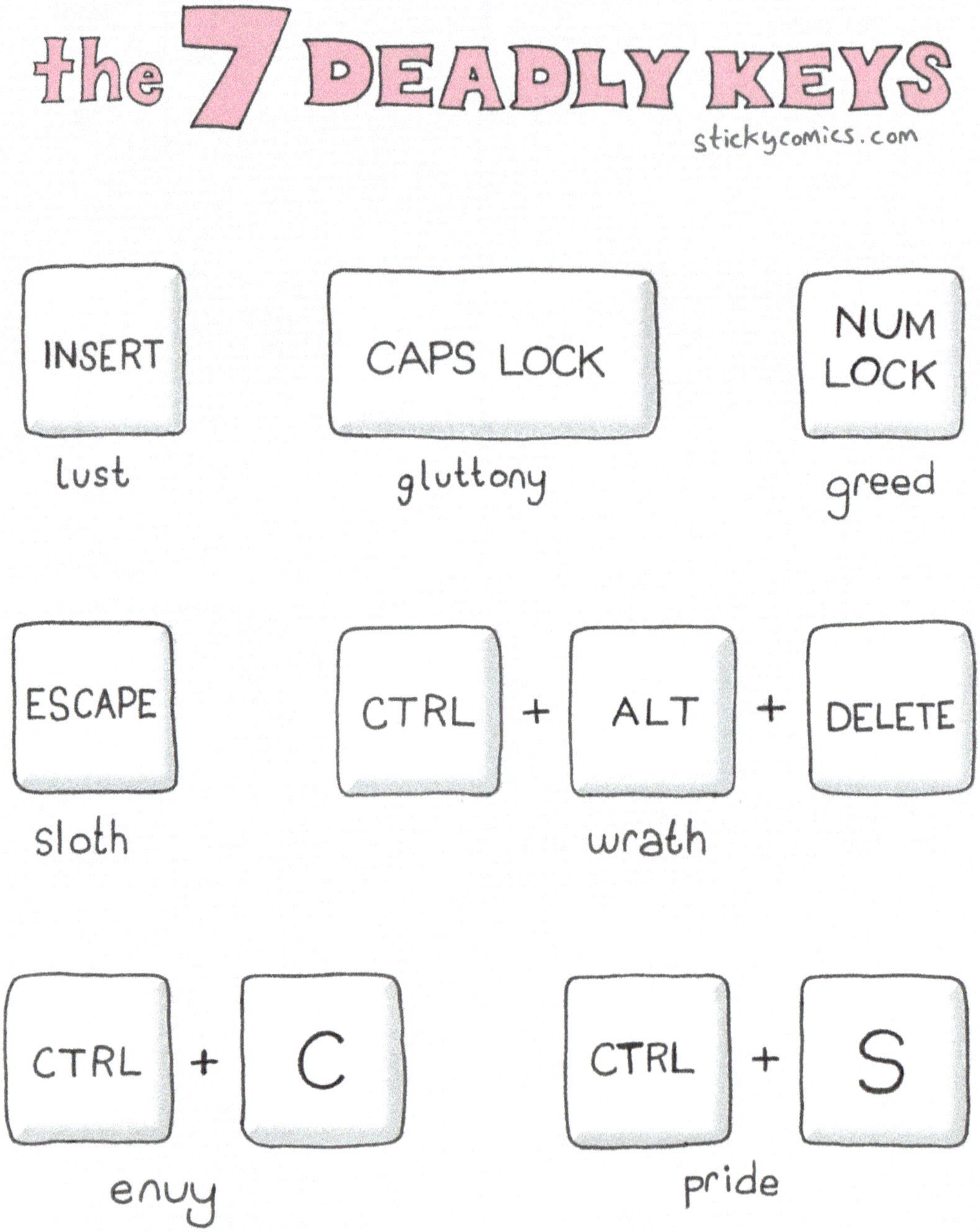

the 7 DEADLY KEYS
stickycomics.com
INSERT
lust
CAPS LOCK
gluttony
NUM LOCK
greed
ESCAPE
sloth
CTRL + ALT + DELETE
wrath
CTRL + C
envy
CTRL + S
pride

Christiann MacAuley - stickycomics.com

TECH GIANTS
WHERE ARE THEY NOW?

2024 stickycomics.com

How we treat our computers...

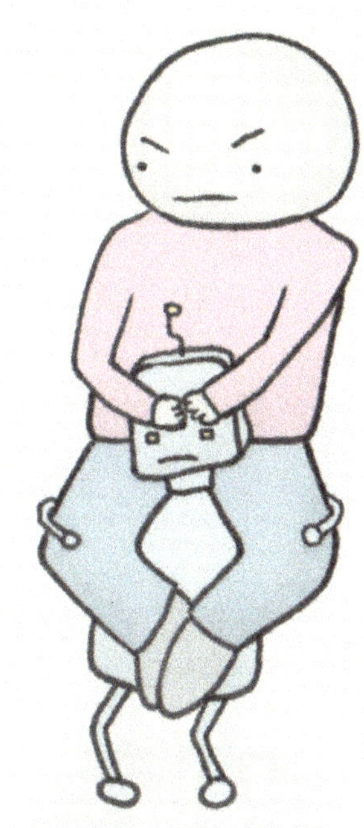

2000
NOBODY READS MY EMAILS.
2005
NOBODY READS MY BLOG
2010
NOBODY READS MY TWITTER
2015
NOBODY READS MY iFace® YouTWEETS
2020
NOBODY READS
stickycomics.com

how to
ANNOY A MILLENNIAL

stickycomics.com

HOW DO YOU CARRY YOUR MOBILE PHONE?

stickycomics.com

WE ARE THE BOOK. YOU WILL BE ASSIMILATED.
Kindle
STICKYCOMICS.COM

PART 9
WHATEVER

WE'LL ALWAYS
HAS CHEEZBURGER

stickycomics.com

HELP!!
I'M BEING ATTACKED BY... !!!?!
OH CRAP HOW DO YOU PLURALIZE THESE THINGS!?!!
stickycomics.com

I'D RATHER BEE KEEPING

AMERICA WAKES UP

sticky comics .com

stickycomics.com

STICKYCOMICS.COM

shit just got real.

THREE... FOUR... FIVE

ZZZZZZZZ

i'M NEVER GONNA FINISH COUNTING THESE THINGS
stickycomics.com

humanists
"We go to church... for the architecture."
stickycomics.com

if pigs
could fly...
my car would be filthy

WELL,
THERE GOES THE
NEIGHBORHOOD
stickycomics.com

POOPIN'
MAKES
YA
OLD
stickycomics.com

i'M WALKIN' ON SUNSHINE!

WHOA HOOOOOOoo!!
stickycomics.com

GOSH IT'S PRETTY OUT TODAY!
THOSE SURFACE VEGGIES ARE SO SHALLOW.
broccoli
tomato
potato
carrots
stickycomics.com

stickycomics.com

stickycomics.com

stickycomics.com
BACATION

this funeral is adorable!
stickycomics.com

burbin' it:
WHEN YOU DON'T NEED
A WINTER COAT BECAUSE
YOUR CAR IS YOUR COAT
stickycomics.com

"tell us another story, grandma!"

"CHOKING HAZARD"?!

IN MY DAY THE "COOLEST" KIDS WERE THE ONES WHO COULD SWALLOW THE MOST TOYS.
stickycomics.com

sick day adventures

stickycomics.com

SPOILER
ALERT
THE
END
IS
NEAR
stickycomics.com

3
TYPES OF PEOPLE
(and a long line)
ooh, i need to get in that line!
how do i cut to the front?
NO WAY, SUCKERS!
stickycomics.com

URBAN STARING

LEARN AND ENJOY!

stickycomics.com

WE'RE
MAGIC
BEANS!!

WOW! DOES THAT
MEAN WE'LL GROW A
MAGIC BEANSTALK?

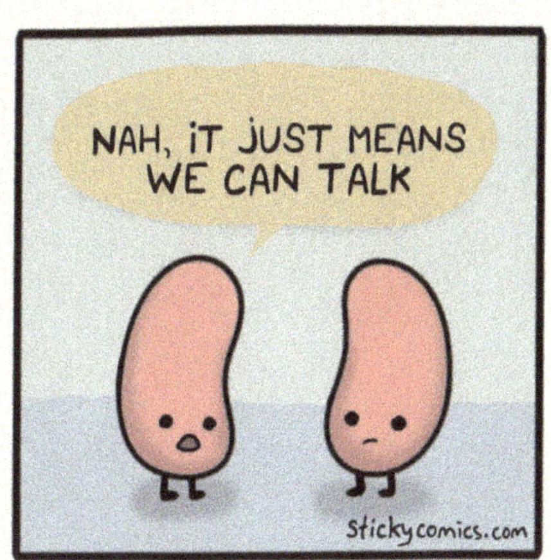

NAH, IT JUST MEANS
WE CAN TALK
stickycomics.com

I HATE BEING
LABELED

YOU MEAN YOU'RE A
NON-CONFORMIST?

DON'T CALL ME
THAT!
stickycomics.com

You know what they call the MIDDLE SEAT
winDON'T expect my help when you have to get up to pee
AiSLE just be over here, minding my own business
stickycomics.com

TYPES OF CLOUDS
a guide
happy little cloud
angry little cloud
serious clouds
cloud squad
artsy clouds
big sad cloud
cloud pretending to be a mountain
cloud wannabes
stickycomics.com

"Grandmother, what big ears you have!"

"The better to hear you with, my dear."

"Grandmother, what big eyes you have!"

"The better to see you with, my dear."

"Grandmother, what big teeth you have!"

"Yes dear...

... Now quiet down and eat your meat."
stickycomics.com

Winning isn't everything

Christiann MacAuley
stickycomics.com
"HEY, CECIL, LET'S NOT TALK POLITICS."

i'm fine
i can get up anytime
i swear
stickycomics.com

my razor's battery died
before i shaved both armpits

at least i tried!
stickycomics.com

THE COUCH
as seen by kids
trampoline
diving platform
pillow
fort
bricks
candy
horde
lava
raft
ammo
free
money
pillow
fort
walls
my spot
mine
also mine
hiding spot
LAVA
the abyss of
all things lost
Stickycomics.com

HAVE YOU
SEEN THIS
SIGN?

HAVE YOU
SEEN THIS
SIGN?

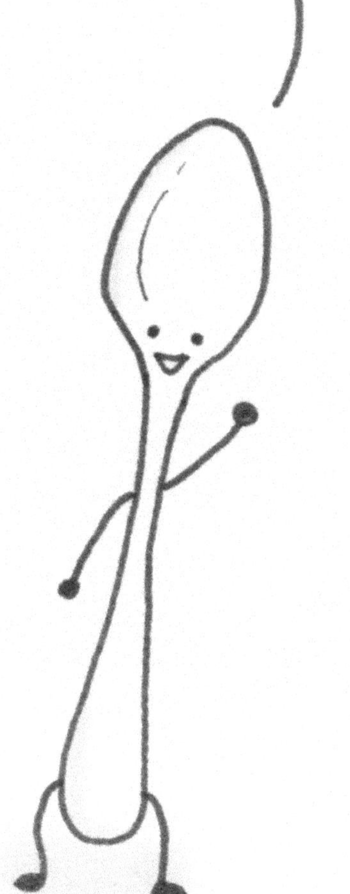

HAVE A KNIFE DAY!
SEE YOU SPOON!
FORK OFF ALREADY!

stickycomics.com

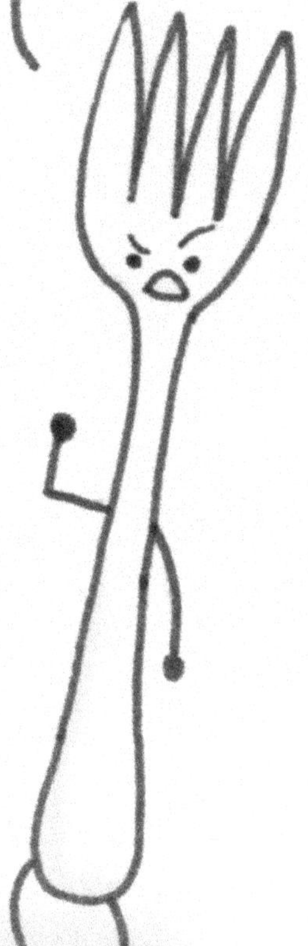

Thanks for reading!

Visit my website & join my email list for
more comics from me on the regular

stickycomics.com